EMMANUEL JOSEPH

The Ripple Effect, How Billionaires Turn Fortunes into Forces of Transformation

Copyright © 2025 by Emmanuel Joseph

All rights reserved. No part of this publication may be reproduced, stored or transmitted in any form or by any means, electronic, mechanical, photocopying, recording, scanning, or otherwise without written permission from the publisher. It is illegal to copy this book, post it to a website, or distribute it by any other means without permission.

First edition

This book was professionally typeset on Reedsy.
Find out more at reedsy.com

Contents

1. Chapter 1: The Genesis of Wealth — 1
2. Chapter 2: Philanthropy and Social Responsibility — 3
3. Chapter 3: Transforming Industries — 5
4. Chapter 4: The Impact on Education — 7
5. Chapter 5: Healthcare Innovations — 9
6. Chapter 6: Environmental Sustainability — 11
7. Chapter 7: Advancing Technology — 13
8. Chapter 8: Economic Empowerment — 15
9. Chapter 9: The Power of Innovation — 17
10. Chapter 10: The Intersection of Wealth and Policy — 19
11. Chapter 11: The Role of Media and Communication — 21
12. Chapter 12: Empowering the Next Generation — 23
13. Chapter 13: Navigating Ethical Dilemmas — 25
14. Chapter 14: The Global Impact — 27
15. Chapter 15: Personal Stories of Transformation — 29
16. Chapter 16: Legacy and Impact — 31
17. Chapter 17: The Future of Billionaire Impact — 33

1

Chapter 1: The Genesis of Wealth

In the tapestry of human history, a select few individuals have amassed wealth on a scale that defies comprehension. The stories of these billionaires often begin humbly, rooted in ordinary beginnings where dreams were the only currency. From the industrious streets of 19th-century New York to the innovative corridors of Silicon Valley, their journeys are marked by relentless perseverance, visionary thinking, and a dash of serendipity. The accumulation of such vast fortunes is not merely a testament to financial acumen but also to the unyielding belief in transforming ideas into reality.

The genesis of wealth for many billionaires is often intertwined with disruptive innovation. Henry Ford revolutionized the automotive industry by introducing assembly line production, making cars affordable for the masses. Similarly, Bill Gates envisioned a world where every household had a personal computer, leading to the Microsoft empire. These pioneers harnessed the power of innovation, turning their ideas into billion-dollar ventures that reshaped entire industries and set the stage for future generations.

Moreover, the early stages of wealth accumulation are characterized by the ability to identify and seize opportunities. Warren Buffett's investment strategies, guided by principles of value investing, exemplify this knack for spotting undervalued assets and turning them into profitable enterprises. Steve Jobs' return to Apple in the late 1990s saw the revival of a nearly bankrupt company into a global tech giant, driven by his unparalleled vision and leadership. These stories underscore the importance of foresight and adaptability in the pursuit of wealth.

Lastly, the genesis of wealth is often accompanied by a profound sense of purpose. For many billionaires, their early experiences and challenges shaped their desire to create something enduring and impactful. Oprah Winfrey's rise from poverty to becoming a media mogul was fueled by her passion for storytelling and empowering others. Through their wealth, these individuals sought not just personal gain but also the opportunity to leave a lasting legacy, setting the stage for the transformative impact they would later have on the world.

2

Chapter 2: Philanthropy and Social Responsibility

As billionaires accumulate vast wealth, a sense of social responsibility often emerges, prompting them to engage in philanthropic endeavors. The concept of wealth as a tool for positive change has gained significant traction, with many billionaires dedicating substantial portions of their fortunes to address pressing global issues. From eradicating diseases to promoting education and environmental sustainability, their philanthropic efforts aim to create a better world for future generations.

One of the most notable examples of billionaire philanthropy is the Bill and Melinda Gates Foundation, established by Bill Gates and his then-wife Melinda. The foundation's mission is to enhance healthcare, reduce extreme poverty, and expand educational opportunities. Through strategic investments and partnerships, the Gates Foundation has made significant strides in combating diseases like malaria and HIV/AIDS, as well as improving access to quality education in underserved communities.

Similarly, Warren Buffett's commitment to philanthropy is exemplified by his pledge to donate the majority of his wealth to charitable causes. In collaboration with the Gates Foundation, Buffett's contributions have amplified the impact of various initiatives aimed at improving global health and education. His emphasis on long-term solutions and sustainable development reflects a deep understanding of the complexities involved in addressing systemic issues.

Beyond individual efforts, the Giving Pledge, co-founded by Gates and Buffett, encourages billionaires worldwide to commit to giving away at least half of their wealth to philanthropic causes. This collective effort has fostered a sense of community among the world's wealthiest individuals, creating a ripple effect that inspires others to use their fortunes for the greater good. By leveraging their resources, influence, and networks, these billionaires are driving meaningful change and setting an example for future generations.

3

Chapter 3: Transforming Industries

Billionaires have an unparalleled ability to transform industries through their innovative thinking and entrepreneurial spirit. Their ventures often disrupt traditional business models, paving the way for new paradigms that redefine how we live and work. From technology to finance, entertainment to healthcare, these individuals have left an indelible mark on various sectors, catalyzing progress and driving economic growth.

In the technology sector, Elon Musk stands out as a visionary entrepreneur who has revolutionized multiple industries. Through companies like Tesla and SpaceX, Musk has advanced the fields of electric vehicles and space exploration. Tesla's commitment to sustainable energy has accelerated the adoption of electric cars, reducing carbon emissions and promoting environmental sustainability. Meanwhile, SpaceX's groundbreaking achievements in reusable rocket technology have lowered the cost of space travel and opened new possibilities for space exploration and commercialization.

In the realm of finance, billionaire investors like George Soros and Ray Dalio have pioneered innovative approaches to investment and risk management. Soros' hedge fund, Quantum Fund, achieved remarkable success through speculative investments and currency trading, influencing global financial markets. Dalio's principles of radical transparency and meritocracy at Bridgewater Associates have redefined corporate culture and investment strategies. Their contributions have shaped the financial landscape, providing valuable insights into navigating the complexities of global markets.

The entertainment industry has also witnessed transformative contributions from billionaires like Oprah Winfrey and Steven Spielberg. Winfrey's media empire, built on her charismatic persona and authentic storytelling, has empowered countless individuals and advocated for social change. Spielberg's groundbreaking films have pushed the boundaries of cinematic art, captivating audiences worldwide and setting new standards for storytelling and visual effects. Their creative vision and entrepreneurial acumen have reshaped the entertainment landscape, leaving a lasting legacy in popular culture.

4

Chapter 4: The Impact on Education

Education is a critical area where billionaires have directed their wealth and influence to create transformative change. Recognizing the power of education in shaping future generations and addressing social inequities, these individuals have invested in initiatives that aim to enhance access to quality education, promote innovation in teaching and learning, and support educational research and development.

One of the most significant contributions to education comes from the philanthropic efforts of the Chan Zuckerberg Initiative, founded by Facebook CEO Mark Zuckerberg and his wife, Priscilla Chan. The initiative focuses on personalized learning, supporting innovative approaches that tailor education to individual student needs. By funding research, technology development, and educational programs, the Chan Zuckerberg Initiative aims to empower students and educators, fostering a more equitable and effective education system.

Similarly, the contributions of billionaires like Laurene Powell Jobs, widow of Apple co-founder Steve Jobs, have made a profound impact on education. Through the Emerson Collective, Powell Jobs has championed educational reform, advocating for policies and practices that address systemic challenges and promote student success. Her investments in educational initiatives, such as college access programs and innovative school models, have provided opportunities for underserved students and driven progress in the education sector.

In addition to funding educational programs, billionaires have also supported the creation of world-class educational institutions. Philanthropist Michael Bloomberg, former mayor of New York City, has made substantial donations to universities and research centers, fostering academic excellence and advancing knowledge in various fields. His contributions to institutions like Johns Hopkins University have enabled cutting-edge research, scholarships, and the development of state-of-the-art facilities, benefitting students and researchers alike.

5

Chapter 5: Healthcare Innovations

Healthcare is another domain where billionaires have leveraged their resources to drive transformative change. Through philanthropic initiatives, investments in medical research, and the establishment of healthcare organizations, these individuals have significantly contributed to advancing medical science, improving patient care, and addressing global health challenges.

The philanthropic efforts of Bill and Melinda Gates in healthcare are unparalleled. Their foundation has funded numerous initiatives aimed at eradicating diseases, improving maternal and child health, and expanding access to essential medicines and vaccines. By partnering with governments, NGOs, and other stakeholders, the Gates Foundation has spearheaded efforts to combat infectious diseases such as polio and malaria, achieving remarkable progress in reducing their prevalence and impact.

In addition to philanthropy, billionaires have also invested in the development of innovative healthcare solutions. Patrick Soon-Shiong, a physician and entrepreneur, has made significant contributions to medical research and biotechnology. Through his company, NantWorks, Soon-Shiong has focused on developing cutting-edge treatments for cancer and other diseases, leveraging advances in genomics and personalized medicine. His work has the potential to revolutionize healthcare, offering new hope to patients and improving outcomes in the fight against life-threatening illnesses.

Moreover, billionaires have supported the establishment of healthcare organizations and facilities that provide high-quality care to underserved populations. Philanthropist Paul Allen, co-founder of Microsoft, established the Allen Institute for Brain Science, which conducts groundbreaking research to understand the complexities of the human brain and develop treatments for neurological disorders. His contributions have advanced scientific knowledge and paved the way for new therapeutic approaches, benefitting patients worldwide.

6

Chapter 6: Environmental Sustainability

Environmental sustainability has become a central focus for many billionaires who recognize the urgent need to address climate change and protect natural resources. Their investments and philanthropic efforts aim to promote renewable energy, conservation, and sustainable practices, driving progress toward a more sustainable future.

One prominent example is the work of Elon Musk, whose ventures in electric vehicles and solar energy have had a significant impact on reducing carbon emissions. Tesla's electric cars and energy storage solutions have accelerated the transition to clean energy, while SolarCity's solar panels have made renewable energy more accessible to households and businesses. Musk's vision for a sustainable future extends beyond Earth, with SpaceX's exploration of reusable rocket technology reducing the environmental footprint of space travel.

In addition to technological innovation, billionaires like Richard Branson have championed environmental conservation through initiatives such as the Virgin Earth Challenge. Branson's commitment to addressing climate change is reflected in his investments in renewable energy, sustainable aviation, and ocean conservation. His advocacy for environmental sustainability has inspired other business leaders and philanthropists to prioritize environmental responsibility in their endeavors.

Moreover, billionaires have supported organizations and initiatives dedicated to environmental research and advocacy. Philanthropist Tom Steyer has focused on promoting climate action through his organization, NextGen America, which advocates for policies to reduce greenhouse gas emissions and transition to clean energy. Steyer's contributions to environmental causes highlight the importance of philanthropy in driving systemic change and fostering a sustainable future.

7

Chapter 7: Advancing Technology

The rapid advancement of technology has been fueled by the investments and innovations of billionaires who push the boundaries of what is possible. Their ventures in artificial intelligence, biotechnology, and space exploration have revolutionized industries and created new opportunities for progress.

Artificial intelligence (AI) has been a key area of focus for billionaires like Larry Page and Sergey Brin, co-founders of Google. Through their investments in AI research and development, Google has become a leader in machine learning, natural language processing, and autonomous systems. AI technologies have the potential to transform various sectors, from healthcare to transportation, by improving efficiency, accuracy, and decision-making.

In the realm of biotechnology, billionaires like Jeff Bezos have invested in companies that aim to extend human lifespan and improve health outcomes. Bezos' investments in biotechnology firms, such as Unity Biotechnology, focus on developing therapies to combat age-related diseases and promote longevity. These advancements in medical science hold the promise of enhancing quality of life and addressing some of the most pressing health challenges.

Space exploration is another frontier where billionaires have made significant contributions. Jeff Bezos' company, Blue Origin, aims to make space travel more affordable and accessible, with the long-term goal of enabling human settlement beyond Earth. Similarly, Elon Musk's SpaceX has achieved remarkable milestones in space exploration, including the first privately-funded spacecraft to reach orbit and the development of reusable rockets. These ventures are paving the way for a new era of space exploration and commercialization.

8

Chapter 8: Economic Empowerment

Economic empowerment initiatives by billionaires aim to create opportunities for individuals and communities to achieve financial independence and improve their quality of life. By investing in entrepreneurship, job creation, and financial inclusion, these efforts seek to address economic disparities and promote sustainable development.

One notable example is the work of billionaire Jack Ma, co-founder of Alibaba Group. Through the Alibaba Foundation and other philanthropic initiatives, Ma has focused on empowering small and medium-sized enterprises (SMEs) by providing access to capital, technology, and markets. His efforts have enabled countless entrepreneurs to grow their businesses, creating jobs and driving economic growth in underserved regions.

Similarly, the philanthropic contributions of George Soros have had a profound impact on economic empowerment. Through the Open Society Foundations, Soros has supported initiatives that promote economic development, social justice, and human rights. His investments in microfinance and social enterprises have provided financial resources and opportunities to marginalized communities, fostering economic resilience and empowerment.

Furthermore, billionaires have championed financial inclusion by supporting initiatives that expand access to banking and financial services. Bill Gates' work with the Gates Foundation includes efforts to promote digital financial inclusion, enabling individuals in developing countries to access and use financial services through mobile technology. These initiatives have empowered millions of people to manage their finances, save for the future, and invest in their livelihoods.

9

Chapter 9: The Power of Innovation

Innovation is a driving force behind the transformative impact of billionaires on society. Their ability to envision new possibilities and bring them to fruition has led to groundbreaking advancements that shape our world. By fostering a culture of innovation and investing in cutting-edge technologies, these individuals have paved the way for progress and growth.

The story of Steve Jobs exemplifies the power of innovation. As co-founder of Apple, Jobs revolutionized the technology industry with iconic products such as the iPhone, iPad, and MacBook. His emphasis on design, user experience, and seamless integration set new standards for consumer electronics and inspired a wave of innovation across the tech sector. Jobs' legacy continues to influence how we interact with technology and has reshaped the way we live, work, and communicate.

In the field of renewable energy, billionaires like Elon Musk have driven innovation to address one of the most pressing challenges of our time: climate change. Tesla's advancements in electric vehicles, energy storage, and solar energy have accelerated the transition to sustainable energy sources. Musk's vision of a sustainable future and his commitment to pushing the boundaries of what is possible have inspired other innovators and entrepreneurs to pursue solutions to global challenges.

Moreover, the pursuit of innovation extends beyond individual efforts, as billionaires often establish organizations and initiatives to foster a culture of creativity and experimentation. The XPRIZE Foundation, founded by Peter Diamandis, offers competitive grants to incentivize technological breakthroughs in fields such as space exploration, healthcare, and environmental sustainability. By challenging innovators to solve complex problems, the XPRIZE Foundation has catalyzed advancements that have the potential to transform industries and improve lives.

10

Chapter 10: The Intersection of Wealth and Policy

Billionaires wield significant influence over public policy, leveraging their resources and networks to shape legislation and advocate for social and economic reforms. Their involvement in policy-making often stems from a desire to address systemic issues and create a more equitable society.

One notable example is the political activism of George Soros, whose Open Society Foundations support initiatives that promote democracy, human rights, and social justice. Soros' efforts to influence policy are driven by his belief in open societies and the importance of government accountability. His contributions to political campaigns, advocacy groups, and think tanks have played a pivotal role in shaping public discourse and driving legislative change.

Similarly, billionaires like Michael Bloomberg have utilized their wealth and influence to advocate for policy reforms in areas such as public health, education, and climate change. Bloomberg's philanthropic initiatives, such as the Bloomberg Philanthropies, support data-driven approaches to policy-making and provide resources to tackle pressing challenges. His advocacy for gun control, tobacco regulation, and climate action has led to significant policy advancements and raised awareness of critical issues.

Moreover, billionaires have formed coalitions and alliances to amplify their impact on policy. The Giving Pledge, co-founded by Bill Gates and Warren Buffett, encourages billionaires to commit to philanthropy and engage in collaborative efforts to address global challenges. Through collective action, these individuals have the potential to influence policy on a larger scale, driving systemic change and promoting social progress.

11

Chapter 11: The Role of Media and Communication

Media and communication play a crucial role in shaping public perception and influencing social change. Billionaires who control media empires have the power to shape narratives, disseminate information, and drive public discourse on important issues.

One prominent example is Rupert Murdoch, whose media conglomerate, News Corp, owns major news outlets such as The Wall Street Journal and Fox News. Murdoch's media empire has played a significant role in shaping public opinion and influencing political landscapes. His control over a vast network of media assets allows him to amplify certain narratives and perspectives, impacting the way people perceive and understand current events.

Similarly, billionaires like Jeff Bezos have ventured into the media industry to leverage their influence and promote quality journalism. Bezos' acquisition of The Washington Post has enabled the newspaper to invest in investigative journalism and expand its digital presence. Under his ownership, The Washington Post has continued to play a vital role in holding power accountable and providing in-depth coverage of critical issues.

Beyond traditional media, billionaires have also invested in digital platforms that facilitate communication and information exchange. Mark Zuckerberg's creation of Facebook revolutionized social media, connecting billions of people worldwide and transforming the way we communicate. Facebook's influence extends beyond social interactions, as it has become a powerful tool for activism, advocacy, and information dissemination. However, the platform's role in spreading misinformation and influencing political outcomes has also raised concerns about its impact on society.

12

Chapter 12: Empowering the Next Generation

Billionaires recognize the importance of investing in the next generation of leaders and innovators. By supporting education, mentorship, and entrepreneurship programs, they aim to empower young people to reach their full potential and drive positive change in their communities.

One notable initiative is the Thiel Fellowship, founded by billionaire Peter Thiel, which provides funding and mentorship to young entrepreneurs who choose to drop out of college to pursue their business ideas. The fellowship aims to encourage innovation and risk-taking, challenging the traditional path of higher education. By supporting young talent, Thiel hopes to inspire a new generation of entrepreneurs who can create transformative solutions to global challenges.

Similarly, the philanthropic efforts of Laurene Powell Jobs through the Emerson Collective focus on empowering young people through education and mentorship. The collective supports initiatives that provide students with the skills and resources needed to succeed in the 21st-century economy. By promoting educational equity and innovation, Powell Jobs seeks to create opportunities for all students to thrive and contribute to society.

Moreover, billionaires have invested in programs that foster leadership and civic engagement among young people. The Obama Foundation, supported by contributions from billionaires like Bill Gates and Michael Bloomberg, aims to inspire and empower young leaders to create positive change in their communities. Through leadership training, mentorship, and networking opportunities, the foundation equips young people with the tools they need to address social challenges and make a meaningful impact.

13

Chapter 13: Navigating Ethical Dilemmas

The immense power and influence wielded by billionaires come with significant ethical responsibilities. As they navigate complex challenges and make decisions that impact society, they must grapple with ethical dilemmas and strive to balance their personal interests with the greater good.

One of the key ethical considerations for billionaires is the source of their wealth. Ensuring that their business practices are fair, transparent, and environmentally sustainable is essential to maintaining public trust and credibility. For example, Elon Musk has faced scrutiny over labor practices at Tesla's factories, prompting calls for improved working conditions and accountability. Addressing these concerns and implementing ethical business practices is crucial for billionaires who seek to create positive change.

Another ethical challenge involves the use of wealth and influence to shape public policy. While billionaires can drive meaningful change through advocacy and philanthropy, their involvement in policy-making raises questions about the concentration of power and the potential for conflicts of interest. Transparency and accountability are essential to ensuring that their efforts are aligned with the public interest and do not undermine democratic processes.

Additionally, the impact of technological innovations on society presents ethical dilemmas for billionaires in the tech industry. Issues such as data privacy, artificial intelligence ethics, and the digital divide require careful consideration and responsible decision-making. Mark Zuckerberg's role in addressing privacy concerns and combating misinformation on Facebook exemplifies the ethical challenges faced by tech billionaires. Striking a balance between innovation and ethical responsibility is critical to ensuring that technological advancements benefit society as a whole.

14

Chapter 14: The Global Impact

The influence of billionaires extends beyond national borders, as their philanthropic initiatives and business ventures have a global reach. By addressing global challenges and fostering international collaboration, they contribute to a more interconnected and resilient world.

One prominent example is the work of the Bill and Melinda Gates Foundation in global health and development. The foundation's initiatives, such as the Global Polio Eradication Initiative and the Gavi Alliance, have made significant strides in reducing disease burden and improving health outcomes in developing countries. By partnering with international organizations, governments, and local communities, the foundation has created a global network of stakeholders committed to advancing health and development.

Similarly, the philanthropic efforts of billionaire Carlos Slim have had a profound impact on economic development and social progress in Latin America. Through the Carlos Slim Foundation, Slim has supported initiatives in education, healthcare, and infrastructure, promoting sustainable development and improving the quality of life for millions of people. His investments in telecommunications have also enhanced connectivity and economic opportunities in the region.

Moreover, billionaires have contributed to global environmental sustainability efforts through initiatives such as the Breakthrough Energy Coalition.

Founded by Bill Gates, the coalition brings together billionaires and investors to fund clean energy research and development. By supporting innovative solutions to climate change, the coalition aims to accelerate the transition to a sustainable energy future and mitigate the global impact of environmental degradation.

15

Chapter 15: Personal Stories of Transformation

Behind the public personas of billionaires lie personal stories of transformation, resilience, and growth. Their journeys are often marked by overcoming adversity, learning from failures, and evolving as leaders and philanthropists.

Oprah Winfrey's rise from poverty to becoming a media mogul is a testament to the power of resilience and determination. Her experiences of overcoming hardship and discrimination have shaped her commitment to empowering others and advocating for social change. Winfrey's personal story of transformation serves as an inspiration to millions, demonstrating that success is attainable through perseverance and a strong sense of purpose.

Similarly, the journey of Amazon founder Jeff Bezos is characterized by continuous innovation and a willingness to embrace failure as a stepping stone to success. Bezos' early ventures, such as the unsuccessful zShops and the Amazon Fire Phone, provided valuable lessons that informed his future endeavors. His ability to learn from setbacks and adapt to changing circumstances has been a driving force behind Amazon's growth and success.

The personal stories of billionaires also highlight the importance of giving back to society. Warren Buffett's decision to pledge the majority of his wealth to philanthropy reflects his belief in using resources for the greater good.

His commitment to humility and ethical responsibility serves as a guiding principle for future generations of leaders and philanthropists.

16

Chapter 16: Legacy and Impact

The legacy of billionaires is often defined by the enduring impact of their contributions to society. Whether through philanthropy, innovation, or policy influence, their efforts leave a lasting imprint on the world, shaping the future for generations to come.

One notable example is the philanthropic legacy of Andrew Carnegie, a 19th-century industrialist who became one of the world's wealthiest individuals. Carnegie's belief in the "Gospel of Wealth" led him to donate the majority of his fortune to charitable causes, including the establishment of libraries, educational institutions, and cultural organizations. His contributions have had a lasting impact on public access to education and knowledge, setting a precedent for modern philanthropy.

Similarly, the legacy of Bill and Melinda Gates continues to inspire future generations of philanthropists. The Gates Foundation's commitment to addressing global health and education challenges has created a ripple effect, encouraging other billionaires to use their wealth for social good. Their emphasis on strategic philanthropy and measurable outcomes has set new standards for charitable giving, ensuring that their impact endures long after their lifetimes.

Moreover, billionaires have left a legacy through their innovative ventures and contributions to technological progress. The advancements made by Steve Jobs, Elon Musk, and other tech visionaries have transformed industries and improved the quality of life for millions of people. Their ability to turn visionary ideas into reality has not only driven economic growth but also inspired future innovators to push the boundaries of what is possible.

17

Chapter 17: The Future of Billionaire Impact

As we look to the future, the impact of billionaires on society is likely to evolve in response to emerging challenges and opportunities. Their ability to drive positive change will depend on their willingness to adapt, collaborate, and remain committed to ethical principles.

One key area of focus for future billionaires will be addressing the global climate crisis. The urgency of climate change requires bold and innovative solutions, and billionaires have the resources and influence to drive meaningful progress. By investing in renewable energy, sustainable practices, and environmental conservation, they can play a pivotal role in mitigating the impacts of climate change and fostering a more sustainable future.

Additionally, the rapid advancement of technology will present both opportunities and ethical challenges for future billionaires. The responsible development and deployment of artificial intelligence, biotechnology, and other emerging technologies will be crucial to ensuring that their benefits are widely shared and do not exacerbate existing inequalities. Future billionaires will need to prioritize ethical considerations and engage in collaborative efforts to address the complex social implications of technological progress.

Furthermore, the future impact of billionaires will be shaped by their commitment to inclusivity and equity. By supporting initiatives that promote diversity, economic empowerment, and social justice, they can help create a more equitable and inclusive society. The continued rise of social entrepreneurship and impact investing will provide new avenues for billionaires to align their wealth with their values and drive positive change.

Ultimately, the future of billionaire impact will be defined by their ability to harness their resources, influence, and vision for the greater good. As they navigate the complexities of a rapidly changing world, their legacy will be measured by their contributions to creating a more just, sustainable, and prosperous future for all.

In "**The Ripple Effect: How Billionaires Turn Fortunes into Forces of Transformation**," we explore the remarkable journeys of the world's wealthiest individuals, delving into how their vast fortunes have become catalysts for positive change. From humble beginnings to disruptive innovation, this book chronicles the genesis of their wealth and the pivotal moments that shaped their success. It uncovers the philanthropic endeavors of billionaires who, driven by a sense of social responsibility, dedicate substantial portions of their wealth to addressing pressing global issues.

The narrative takes readers through the transformative impact billionaires have on various industries, from technology and finance to healthcare and entertainment. Their visionary thinking and entrepreneurial spirit redefine traditional business models, paving the way for new paradigms. We also delve into their contributions to education, healthcare, and environmental sustainability, highlighting how their resources and influence drive meaningful progress in these critical areas.

As we navigate the ethical dilemmas and global challenges faced by billionaires, we see how their commitment to inclusivity, equity, and responsible innovation shapes their legacy. Through personal stories of resilience, leadership, and philanthropy, the book illustrates the profound impact these individuals have on society. Ultimately, "The Ripple Effect" provides a compelling look at how billionaires harness their wealth to create a more just, sustainable, and prosperous future for all.

www.ingramcontent.com/pod-product-compliance
Lightning Source LLC
LaVergne TN
LVHW020459080526
838202LV00057B/6051